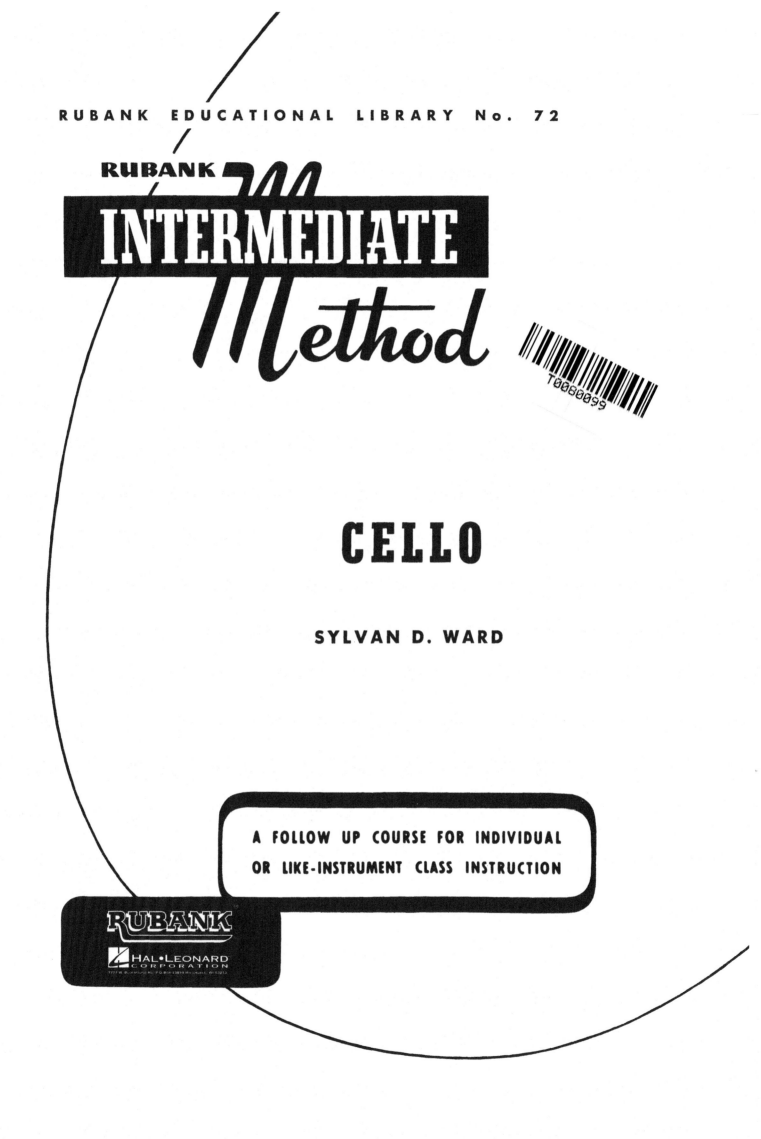

RUBANK EDUCATIONAL LIBRARY No. 72

RUBANK

INTERMEDIATE

Method

CELLO

SYLVAN D. WARD

A FOLLOW UP COURSE FOR INDIVIDUAL
OR LIKE-INSTRUMENT CLASS INSTRUCTION

RUBANK

HAL•LEONARD
CORPORATION
7777 W. BLUEMOUND RD. P.O. BOX 13819 Milwaukee, WI 53213

Bowings and Effects Used in Orchestra and Solo Playing

Bowing may be analyzed with the discussion of three fundamental strokes:

1. *The sustained stroke:* Italian — sostenuto;   French — soutenu.

2. *The hammered stroke:* Italian — martellato;   French — martelé.

3. *The springing, bouncing or rebounding stroke:* Italian — spiccato or saltato;   French — sautillé.

There are several types of bowings which are identified with the Sustained Stroke.

1. *The Full Bow, or Full Arm Stroke* is one of the most valuable strokes and probably the least used by students. This requires the bow's entire length with full cooperation of the wrist, elbow and shoulder joints. Care should be taken to move the bow parallel with the bridge. Mastery of the Full Bow Stroke solves many bowing problems and results in accurate interpretation of dynamics. In Sustained passages it requires considerable skill to connect the tones as the bow changes at the point and at the frog. The fingers and wrist play the important part in connecting the tones. When notes are marked legato with lines above, the full bow is usually used, but in most cases music is not marked and bowing is left to the discretion of the conductor or the player.

2. *The Sustained Wrist Stroke* calls for manipulation usually at the middle of the bow (abbreviated M). The strokes are very short, about one inch or less. Performed at rapid speed the stroke results in a bounding bow if a flexible wrist is maintained. The Bounding Stroke is described later.

Sight reading is retarded immeasurably in the orchestra because string players are unable to associate certain groups of notes or rhythmical patterns with a specific style of bowing. Bowing practice makes identification quicker and students should spend much time in home practice, breaking up scales in rhythmic patterns that will offer a variety of bowings. The following are suggested, many of which call for the Sustained Stroke in the upper half of the bow (abbrev. U.H.) and lower half (abbrev. L.H.) demanding great flexibility of arm and wrist, and permitting varying degrees of intensity of tone:

Practice these bowings with the use of different Scales.

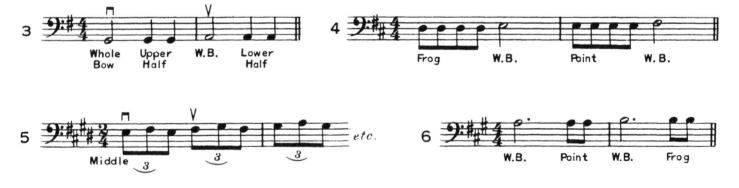

Use the same amount of bow for each note without making the second tone sound louder than the first.

Copyright MCMXLII by Rubank, Inc., Chicago, Ill.
International Copyright Secured

Practice first at lower half of bow, then at the middle portion and finally at the upper half.

The *Hammered Stroke (Detached or Martele)* is a heavy, quick stroke which allows for no gradu- ation in dynamics. It is performed at the point, usu- ally with about three to six inches of the bow. The

forearm is jerked very rapidly, coming to a quick stop for each note. The violent jerking of the forearm is ac- companied with a pinching of the bow with the right hand. This, with the relaxation of the hand at the end of each stroke, produces the desired effect. The stroke is sometimes indicated with peculiar marks over the notes but more often the music itself suggests the stroke.

The *sforzando (sfz)* is also performed by quick pressure plus pinching of the stick and then immediate relaxation. The tonal effect is of a *ff* followed immediately by a *pp*. If the note is short, the effect is of a sharp accent.

Other variations of the Hammered Stroke are: the *Grand Detache*, the same as martelé but re- quires more bow; the *Staccato or Solid Stacca- to,* a very brilliant stroke, most often executed at the middle of the bow. The bow remains solidly on

the string and does not lift as in the springing staccato bowing. It is also performed with two or many more notes in one bow, stopping the bow for each note. This is probably the most difficult stroke known. It is u- sually done with an up-bow but frequently appears as a down-stroke.

When the music calls for a graceful, wistful, capricious, will-o'-the-wisp style, the springing bow usually comes in- to play under the classification of *Natural Spiccato.* The stroke is very light, performed most effectively at the mid- dle of the bow with flexible wrist and bow hair flat on strings. Very little of the bow is used and as it is jerked back and forth freely, it bounds on its own momentum. Perpetual Motions usually require this kind of bowing.

4

The other kind of springing bow is the *Artificial Spiccato*, more of a controlled stroke done, not with the wrist alone, but with the entire arm. Because of the cumbersome nature of this stroke,

the staccato passages are slower in tempo than those interpreted by the Natural Spiccato bowing. The variants of the Artificial Spiccato are the Sustained Spiccato Stroke and the Hammered Spiccato. To perform the *Hammered Spiccato*, the bow is held firmly with the fingers and allowed to strike the strings viciously near the frog, so that the notes sound dry, crisp and abrupt.

The *Sustained Spiccato* has quite a different tonal effect because the bow strikes the string in a more graceful, sweeping manner so that the tone is more sustained. This bowing finds much use in or-

chestra and in solo performance. The spiccato is very seldom marked in music. The kind of bowing to select is usually determined by the character and tempo of the music.

The *Ricochet or Thrown Staccato* applies to two or more staccato notes connected in one bow. The upper part of the bow is used. The bow is raised rather high and thrown on the string so

that it is allowed to rebound the exact number of notes needed. *Col Legno* is a Thrown Staccato Stroke using the stick and the hair together. It applies to single notes, or double stops (two or more notes played at one time). The bow is dropped on the string almost perpendicularly.

The *Arpeggio Stroke* is a succession of notes in arpeggio form bounding over three or four strings by means of the Natural Spiccato. Very little bow is used and is played at the middle.

The *Tremolo* is a very fast stroke (alternating down and up bows, short and speedy) usually exe-cuted at the point of the bow and is capable of giv-ing a very startling effect in the orchestra. It lends itself well to pianissimos and stirring crescendos.

The *Pizzicato*. When performing rapid passages it is usually desirable to alternate the index and second fingers. However, some players find it just as easy to use the index finger only, with of course a free wrist motion. The thumb of the right hand is not placed against the edge of the fingerboard except in slow, deliberate passages.

In passages of double notes play the notes simultaneously with the thumb and index finger. The thumb plays the low note and the index finger the top one.

Pizzicato chords, of three or four notes, are played by brushing the thumb gracefully over the strings, starting from the lower string. Do not go directly across the strings but rather move diagonally, lifting the hand as it strikes the top note.

Two Melodies in Fourth Position

Test with Open G string
to be sure you have the right note

1st Pos.

1st Position

Fingerings for 4th Position, Key of G Major (∨ means half step)

C string   G string   D string   A string

Key of C Major

Remember the rule: When there are 2 consecutive whole steps between 1st and 4th fingers, use 1-2-4 fingering.

Preparatory Study for Double Stops and Chords

Keep the fingers down

Arpeggios

Chords

Also play this last line Pizzicato, using the right thumb.

For Instructions on playing pizzicato, see page 4.

Melody in Third Position

poco ritard.

Fingerings for 3rd Position, Key of A Major.

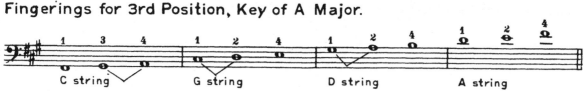

C string   G string   D string   A string

Crossing the Strings in Third Position

Remain in 3rd Position

1st Pos.   3rd Pos.   *rit.*

Double Stops in Third Position.

Play the E♭ Major Scale first to get the feel and sound of the key.

Also play the above two lines on the C and D strings in the Key of A♭; also on the D and A strings in the Key of B♭ Major.

Fingerings for 3rd Position, Key of E♭ Major.   **Fingerings in B♭ Major.**

Melody in Second Position

Double Stops in Second Position.

Also play the above two lines on the G and D strings in the Key of D♭; also on the C and G strings in the Key of G♭ Major.

Fingerings for 2nd Position, Key of F Major.   Fingerings in Key of A♭ Major.

The Harmonic

The Harmonic is a flute-like tone which is obtained by stopping the string lightly with the finger. Natural Harmonics appear in various places in the string. The most commonly used is the octave Harmonic which divides the string exactly in half from nut to bridge. This is usually played with the 3rd finger by extending the finger up from fourth position. The Harmonic is indicated by a cipher along with the finger to be used $\binom{4}{0}$.

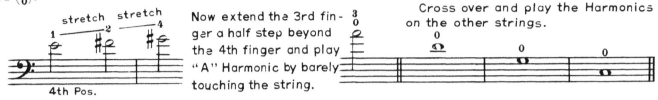

Now extend the 3rd finger a half step beyond the 4th finger and play "A" Harmonic by barely touching the string.

Cross over and play the Harmonics on the other strings.

When playing the Harmonic be sure not to allow the hand or arm to rest on the body of the instrument.

For practice, use different fingerings. For example, play all of the ascending notes with the 1st finger, then the 2nd, then the 3rd finger. Think of your positions so you can make the shifts accurate. Also practice slurring 2 notes in a bow.

Playful Harmonics

Theme and Variation

Always look at your key signature first to determine where your half steps and whole steps are going to be.

The Turn (∾)

The Turn is a form used to represent a group of notes played before or after a note thus:

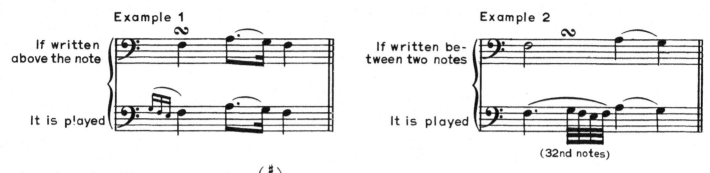

If a sharp is written above the Turn (∾#) the highest note is raised.

If a sharp is written below the Turn (∾#) the lowest note is raised.

If a flat is written, the note would be lowered.

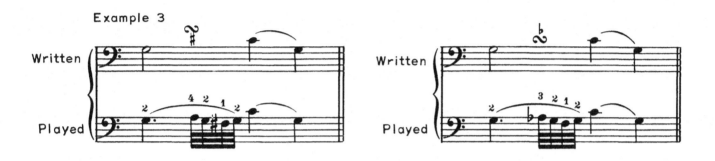

Shepherd's Tune

The Old Spinning Wheel Hums a Tune

Note: To develop smooth bowing, practice the first three lines and the last three lines with 8 notes in one bow.

Merry Dance

Learning to Recognize Intervals

A cellist should acquire the habit of hearing notes mentally before playing them. This practice e-liminates much guess work, faulty reading, and bad intonation. A good knowledge of Intervals is indispens-able in sight reading. When you know the relationship of one note to another a mental picture is formed where otherwise the notation may be meaningless. After you have learned the exact names of the Intervals, try singing them. You may be surprised how quickly your inner ear grasps the tones so that hearing Intervals comes as natural as the mechanics of playing them. Practice carefully and patiently. Don't expect a mira-cle. At this point it is assumed you know the names of the sharps and flats in the major scale. If you do not, refresh your memory by studying pages 42-44.

The General Names of Intervals

The general name of an Interval is found by counting the lines and spaces (or letter names) included by the two notes. For example, the first line on the staff is G and the first space is A. We learn the In-terval between these two notes by counting the lines and spaces. G is the first line and A is the adjoining space so the Interval is a "second". Or, if you wish to count letter names, G is the first letter and A is the second so the Interval is a "second". Others are as follows:

| Unison | Second | Third | Fourth | Fifth | Sixth | Seventh | Octave | Ninth | Tenth |

To determine the exact name of an Interval, simply think of the lower note as being the name of a ma-jor scale. For example, if the lower note is D, think of the D major scale. If the upper note belongs to the scale, the Interval is "major", except in the case of octaves, fifths, fourths, and unisons, for which the term "perfect" is used.

| Perfect Unison | Major Second | Major Third | Perfect Fourth | Perfect Fifth | Major Sixth | Major Seventh | Perfect Octave | Major Ninth | Major Tenth |

If the upper note does not belong to the scale named by the lower note, the following considerations are ap-plied.
1. An Interval a half-step smaller than a major Interval is "minor".
2. An Interval a half-step larger than a major or a perfect Interval is "augmented".
3. An Interval a half-step smaller than a minor or a perfect Interval is "diminished".

The Interval G to A♭ is not a major second because A♭ is not a member of the G major scale. To be major, the top note would have to be A♮. Since it is A♭ it would make the Interval a half-step short of being a major and would therefore be correctly named a MINOR SECOND.

The Interval G to A♯ is a half step larger than a major second so will be correctly named an AUGMENTED SECOND.

The Interval G to D♭ is not a perfect fifth because the top note is not in the scale of the lower note. The Interval is a half step smaller than the perfect so would be called a DIMINISHED FIFTH.

Interval Practice*

Practice pizzicato first, then with the bow.

SECONDS

Major Second   Minor Second   Major Second   Major Second   Minor Second

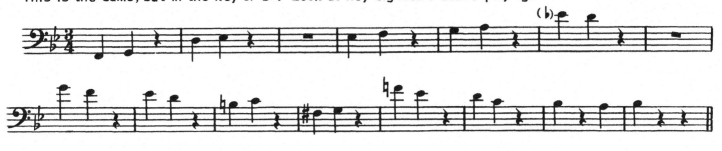

This is the same, but in the key of B♭. Look at key signature before playing.

THIRDS

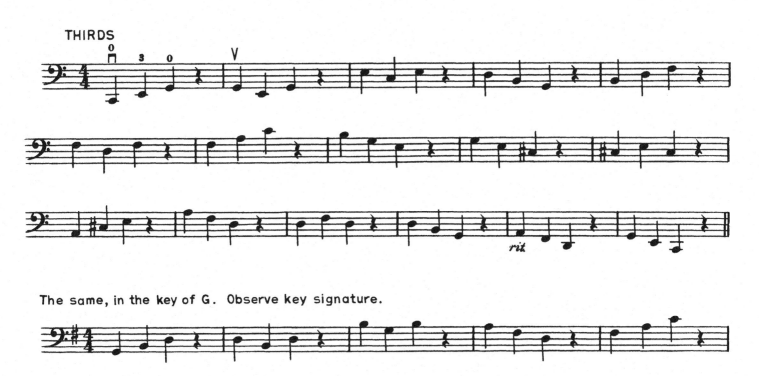

rit.

The same, in the key of G. Observe key signature.

rit.

★ ① Name the exact intervals before playing them.
② Play the first note in each measure then sing the remaining notes.

18

Name the intervals before playing.

FOURTHS

4th Position

The same, in the key of A♭. Look at signature carefully before playing.

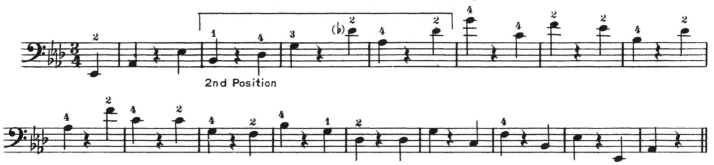

2nd Position

FIFTHS

Note change of signature.

4th Position

Practice three ways: *frog, middle, point.*

SIXTHS

Study key signature carefully. Name all of the notes in the piece.

SEVENTHS

OCTAVES

NINTHS

Continue back downward

Return downward

TENTHS

Return downward

4th Pos.

Return downward

Review of Half Position

Point out the Half Steps before playing.

Double Stops in Half Position.

Detached Bowing Melody

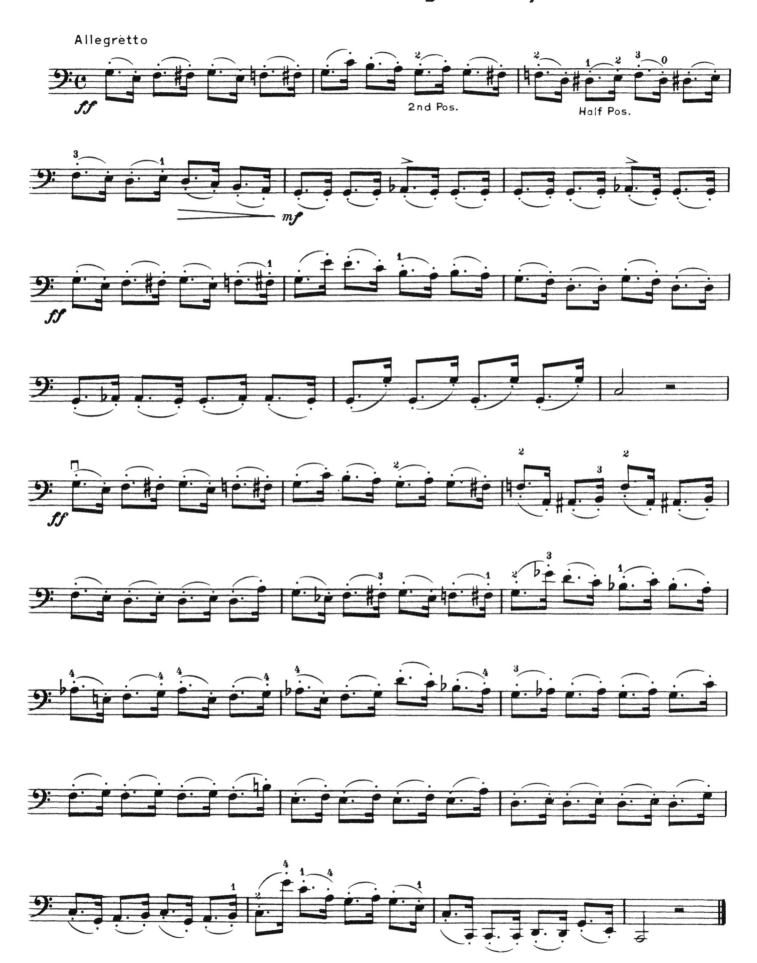

Sailing Along

Theme in F Major

Melody with Shifts into 2nd, 3rd & 4th Positions

1/2 Pos.

2nd Pos.

Somber Woods

Remain in 3rd Position

ritard. and calando

Langsam

Fingerings for 3rd position, Key of C Minor.

C String   G String   D String   A String

Ricochet Bowing★

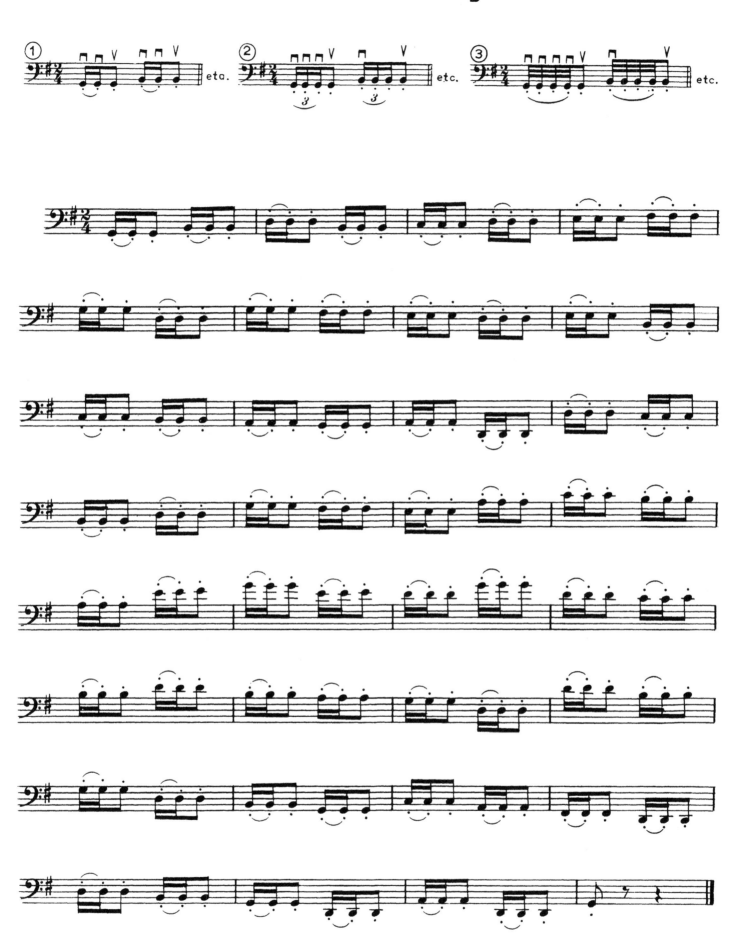

★ See this and other bow strokes described on pages 2, 3 and 4.

Power in the Bow

★ Martelé stroke — The bow is moved quickly and stopped abruptly.

★ See this and other important bow strokes on pages 2, 3 and 4.

Easy Pickin'

Scherzo

Also play the number pizzicato.

912 - 51

In Olden Times

Slowly, in Minuet style

Feathertouch

Triplets Play a Tune

Also practice accenting. First play the piece with the accent (>) on the 1st note of each triplet, then on the 2nd note and finally on the last note.

Breakwater

Also practice the Etude with these bowings:
and others you can think of.

Empire Builder

Note: This sign ? means use the thumb. To simplify the stretch required in playing consecutive octaves, it is customary to use the thumb in place of the 1st finger. In the above notation, the note is G. Place the side of your thumb on top of the string (in third position) and the note "G" will sound. The octave G will be played by the 3rd finger on the A string.

Arpeggi
(Broken Chords)

Practice: ① Separate bowing, ② Two in a bow, ③ Three in a bow, ④ Six in a bow.

Famous Kreutzer Etude

Practice with many different bowings.

Allegro moderato

Concert Waltz

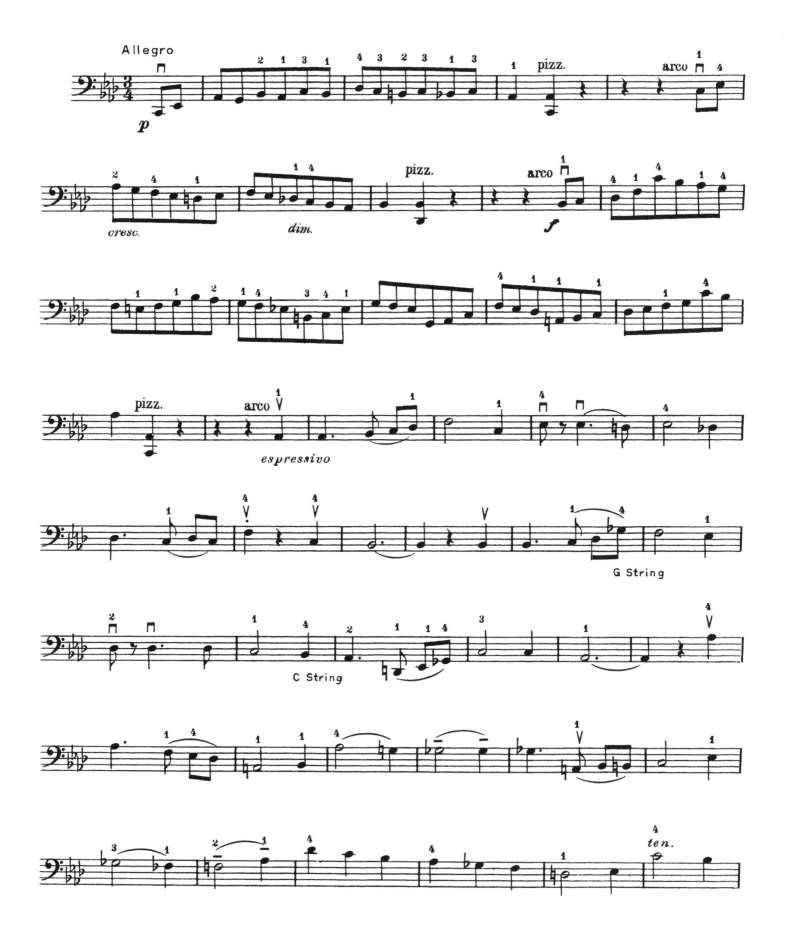

Introducing the Tenor Clef

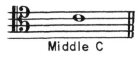

Middle C

You will notice that Middle C appears on the 4th line in tenor clef. The clef is made by taking three lines from the bass clef and one line from the treble clef with Middle C occupying the other line.

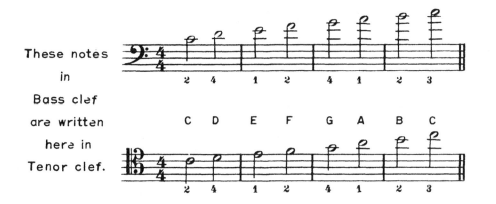

These notes in Bass clef are written here in Tenor clef.

C D E F G A B C

In examining the two lines above you will notice that the tenor clef brings some of the notes down into the staff, thus eliminating notes with many leger lines that are difficult to read. Study the notes and fingering carefully so you will be able to recognize and play them when you see the change of clef in solos and orchestra music.

Here is a 2-octave scale showing how the Bass clef connects with the Tenor clef.

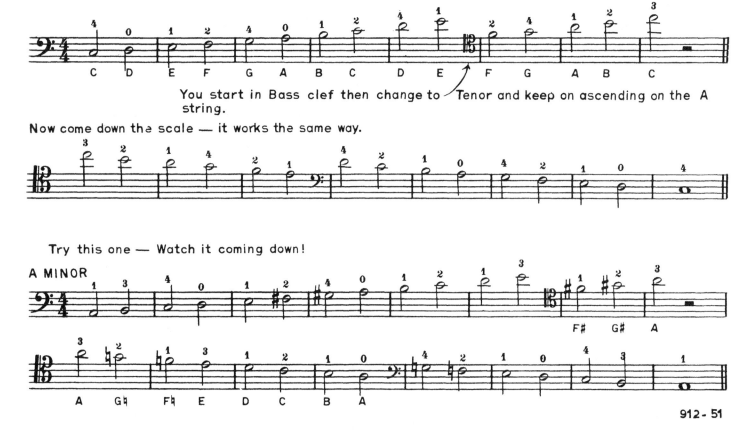

C D E F G A B C D E F G A B C

You start in Bass clef then change to Tenor and keep on ascending on the A string.

Now come down the scale — it works the same way.

Try this one — Watch it coming down!

A MINOR

F# G# A

A G♮ F♮ E D C B A

Four Familiar Melodies

Name the notes before playing.

Fine (end)

D. S. al Fine
(Go back to 𝄋 and end
at "Fine")

912-51

Major Scales in Two and Three Octaves

Practice slowly and play each note very rhythmically. Work for perfect intonation then the speed of scales may be gradually increased. To avoid monotony, practice the scales with different types and styles of bowing; For example: two notes in one bow, four in a bow, eight notes in a bow. After slurring the notes, try them detached, ie., stopping the bow for each note (staccato). Think of your half steps and whole steps as you practice, then the key signature will take on some significance. Don't play merely by ear as this involves too much guess work and limits sight reading ability.

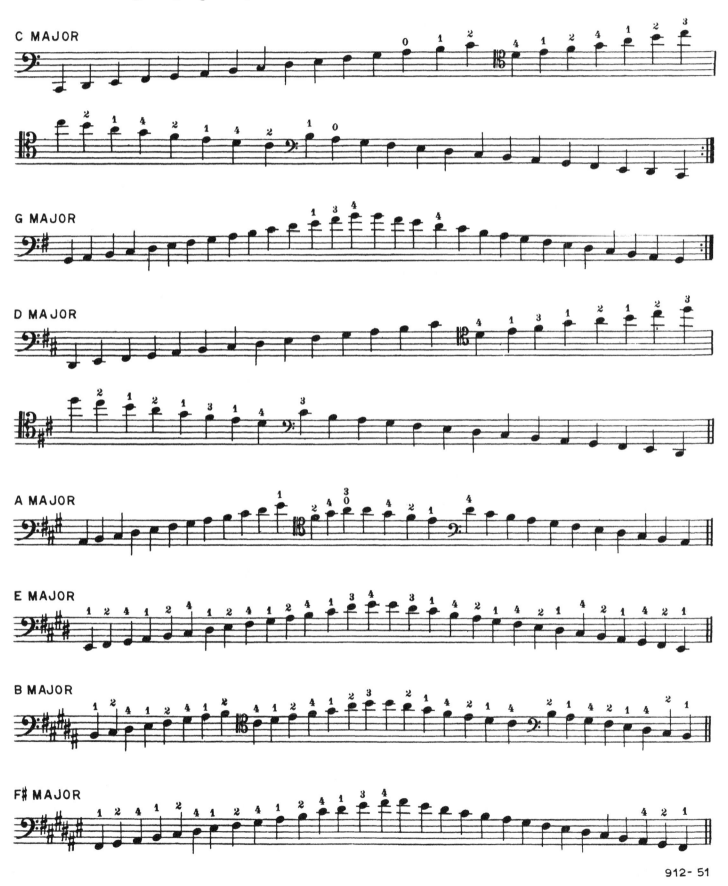

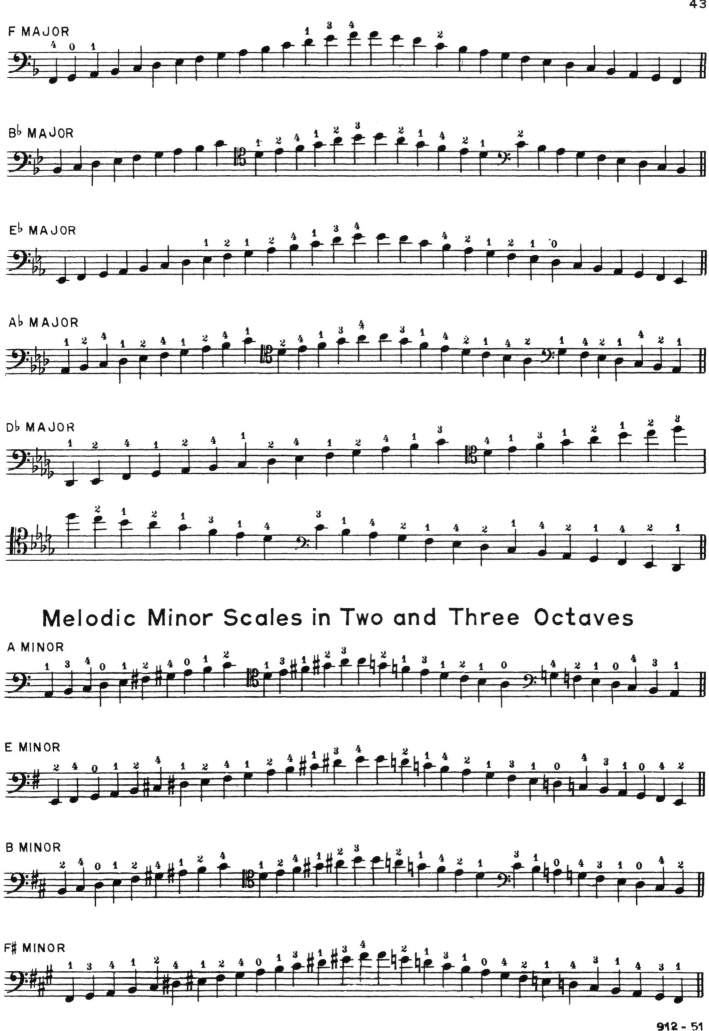

Melodic Minor Scales in Two and Three Octaves

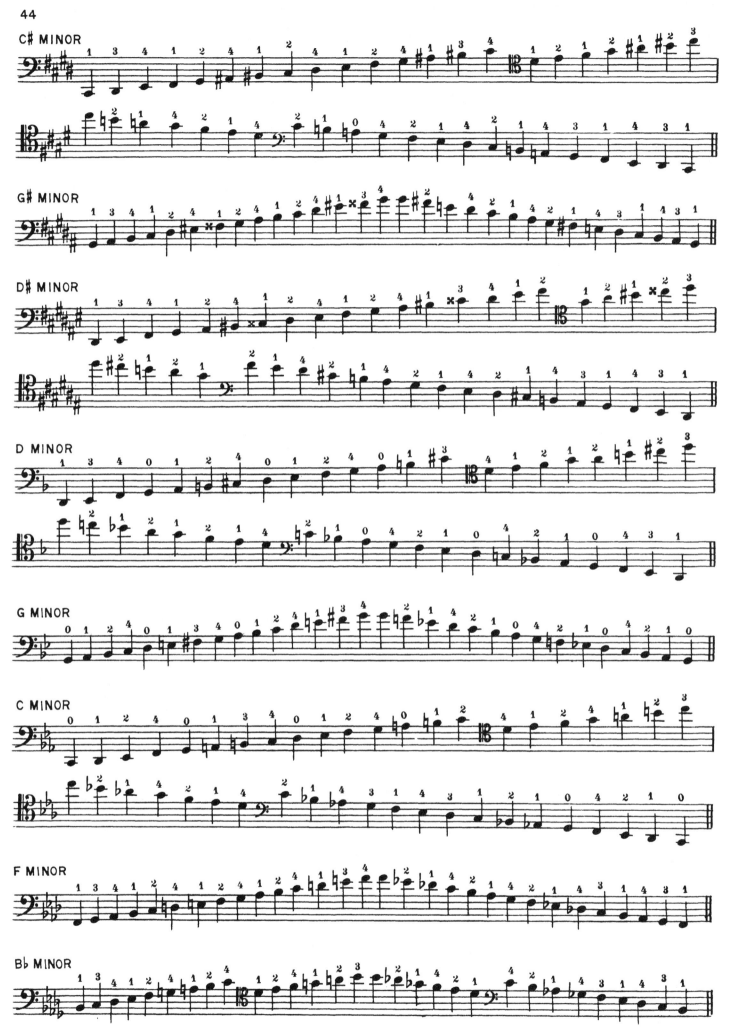

Making Tenor Clef Easy to Read

Name the notes before playing.

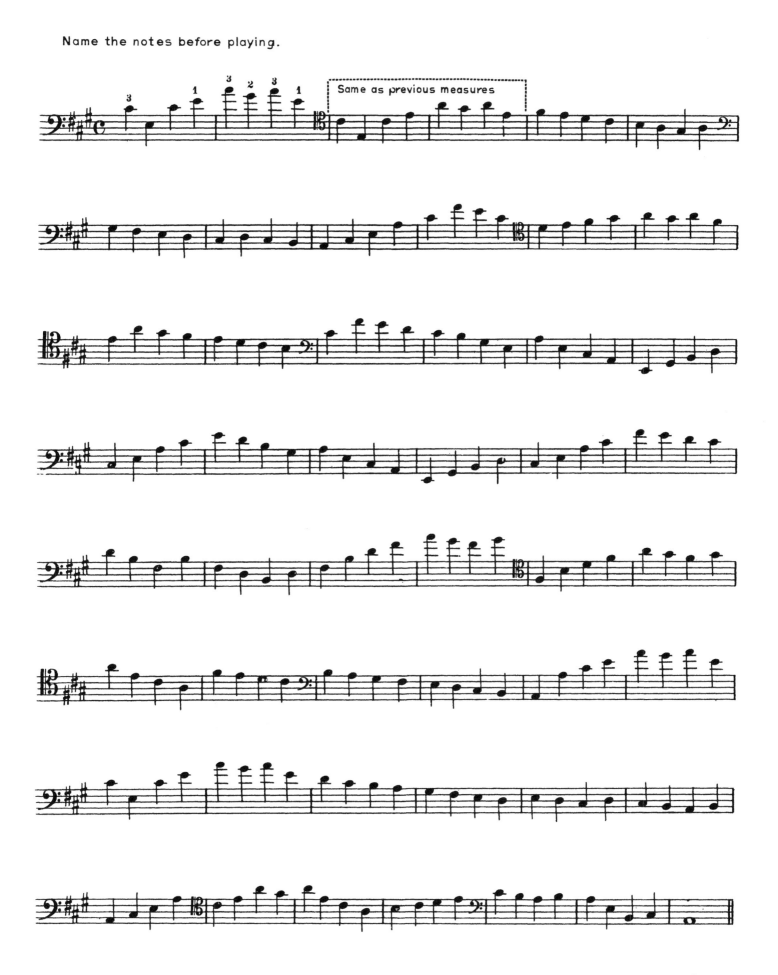

Three Melodies in Syncopation

Preliminary Practice. Try each of the following rhythms on a scale.

Syncopating Novelty

The Famous Cello Solo from
Beethoven's 5th Symphony

1st Symphony

The Young Prince and the Young Princess
from Rimsky-Korakoff's "Scheherazade"

Midsummer Night's Dream
Excerpt from Mendelssohn

Intermezzo
Duet for Two Cellos

Cello I

Intermezzo
Duet for Two Cellos

Cello II

The Three Clefs

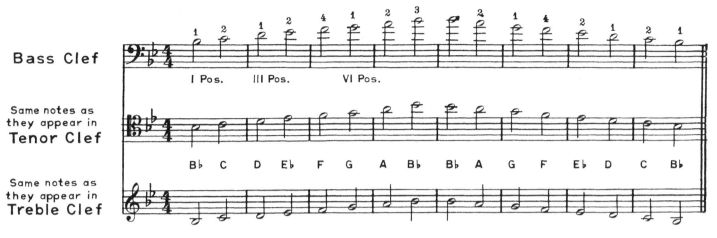

Bass Clef

I Pos.   III Pos.   VI Pos.

Same notes as they appear in **Tenor Clef**

B♭ C D E♭ F G A B♭ B♭ A G F E♭ D C B♭

Same notes as they appear in **Treble Clef**

The Thumb Position

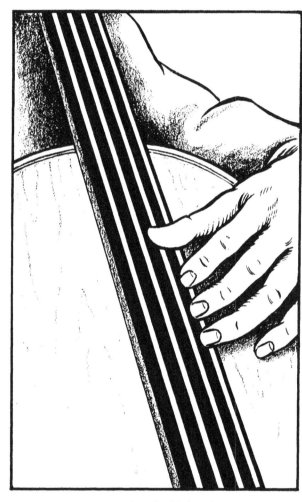

Playing on the **A String**

In order to facilitate passage work in the higher positions, the thumb positions are brought into use. The first thumb position is shown in the illustration and starts in the middle of the string where the octave harmonic is found.

The outer edge of the thumb is placed across two strings in such a manner that the higher string is stopped by the middle joint, and the lower string at the root of the nail. The use of the thumb makes it possible to play full scales across the strings without leaving the position.

These high notes using the thumb positions are usually written in treble clef. The symbol used for the thumb is ♀.

A string Harmonic   D string Harmonic

Press the side of the thumb down on the A and D strings where the 3rd finger played the Harmonics.

A B C♯ D D C♯ B A

Move over to the D string